www.finishinglinepress.com

The Toothmakers' Daughters

poems by

Katherine Fallon

Finishing Line Press
Georgetown, Kentucky

The Toothmakers' Daughters

ACKNOWLEDGMENTS

An earlier version of "Apprenticeship" was published in October 2015 by *GERM* magazine, under the title "The Tooth Makers' Daughter is Apprenticed."

Publisher: Leah Maines

Editor: Christen Kincaid

Cover Art and Design: Lauren Duguid
        Cover art images sourced from *Dental crowns* and
        Illustration of teeth and roots
        Credit: Wellcome Collection. CC BY

Author Photo: Megan Mercer

Printed in the USA on acid-free paper.
Order online: www.finishinglinepress.com
        also available on amazon.com

Author inquiries and mail orders:
Finishing Line Press
P. O. Box 1626
Georgetown, Kentucky 40324
U. S. A.

Table of Contents

For Leah, who has always made me plural

The Toothmakers' Daughters' Mouths Make Room

After learning we didn't have to
wait for loss and that loss

would bring us fortune,
we set to work, loosing.

The Toothmakers' Daughter, Learning to Speak

When my front tooth fell out,
rough as a sand dollar at the rift,

I dreamed of eating from a tray
of glass cakes. The tooth autotomized—

caught leg of a centipede—and a sugar rose
shone at me, proud. They would have me

believe I am afraid of losing
power. Or beauty. Or someone

I love. That I suffer, am not fed enough
by my own hand. That my tongue's

a mute worm: something I need
to say but don't.

Apprenticeship

Father taught us that teeth bloom
like flowers, spiraling outward
from a tight bud. Or like a lady's skirt

mid-dance. But he showed me with his fist,
held so closely to my face that I was forced
to watch it break:

a pale and noiseless fusillade.

The Toothmakers' Daughters, Leaving Home

Eye pressed so close to the peephole that lashes
rustle like wings of fugitive birds. Screen door gutted

by cat claws, impatience, thunderstorm beatings.
Each door opens to the porch, as dark as the room

it led from, dusty switch plate a carved wooden molar—
on as live inside the wall as a tangled rope of nerve.

Always unlocked, the hip must bruise against solid wood
to startle the latch into unfastening.

The Toothmakers' Daughter, Learning to Eat

Teeth as ghostwritten journals:
you can see that once, I was one

of four and later, I belonged as half
of a set of two. Candlesticks flanking

supper. A pair of soft-soled shoes.
I was loved once, and fed plenty.

You will recognize feast, feast,
feast. And after feast, famine.

Prodigal Daughter

Two root canals at twenty-one, two more at twenty-six.
The frozen walkways shone whitely while I slept inside
my pain. At thaw, I flew home to ask for help.

Hurt a homing device, my need greater than my will,
my jaw a row of seats gradually emptying to make room.
If not for their touch, for their trade.

Trophy Hunter

I warn the dentists every time. Nerves like bypasses,
curved as scythes. One man saw my mouth as litmus,
a true test of his mettle.

The glowing x-ray—the clean-limned, phantom jellyfish
of his needling and scraping efforts—was deserving
of the wall above the mantel. Even he failed.

They never believe me. The roots go deeper
than they think, and, in dying, make noise.

The Toothmakers' Daughter, Learning to Love

Dead at the root, they drilled it down
to a sharp shape like a desert plateau,

then made a model of my mouth to fit
the counterfeit. I gave it to a woman,

who knocked it from our nightstand reaching
for a glass of water. Dust fanned across

the hardwoods. The model cracked
along its squeaking hinge.

The Toothmakers' Daughter, Learning to Speak II

Rest and hold your tongue
beneath the dam, still and not
unlike a wetted ribbon. Best

not think about the drill's
descent, or the pulp, all spoiled
and hot. Do not flinch or fold

like a bellows, his forearm
atop your sternum: he uses you
to steady himself, and for your own

good. Spit when told to, raise a hand
if you feel pain.

Allegiance

At the dentist's, the machine beside me boasts
that it can create a crown from an impression
in a matter of hours. Soon I'll have the third tooth

crafted by my parents cemented into place
over the gutted roots. I try not to meet
the machine's digital glare. I feel responsible.

I mustn't ever tell them that I had a choice, and that
for a moment, I thought to opt for ease.

Initiation

The first night I left the table
to drape myself above the toilet,
I knew it was something I would do

over and over for my family, a way inside
a fold I felt myself always outside of.
After I vomited a bottle of wine into the bowl

I returned to the table, lit a cigarette, fingered
the bitten tip of my father's spent cigar.

Crux

Down south, Mother was awakened from years
of much-needed sleep. Higher than a mountain,
then fallen. She closed up around the thermometer
like a collapsible tent. One more drink or one more
dry hour and we'd have buried her, an empty tin.

Breach

Her teeth broke my father's skin
and he sent me away before calling

for help. I passed the wailing ambulance
on the road that led to our unlocked house.

We believed always if someone found
our home among the trees, they'd have earned

what they took from us.

The Toothmakers' Daughter, Reacting

When Mother fell again into seizure, set off a noise
in the joints of her metal bed, same as rattling teeth,

a pan of stones, I did what I'd watched my father do:
slid my hand into her mouth, let her bite my finger

to protect her tongue. Then the nurse rushed in
and I was removed from her side, was pushed.

Home Free

Muscadine, scuppernong, garden-
variety grape-rot: she'll not go near
it again. I thought I recognized her

dying day, when the wind—nuisance child—
lifted the table glass from its curling
haunches and shook it loose into

the shivering pampas grass. Loads
of manure sat shadowed as shot horses,
a green unwanted thriving within. . .

The Toothmakers' Daughters, Marking Time

Mother, a worn workman's glove
on the bus bench, ring finger folded

into the dirty, unlined palm. Counting up
to the fourth multiple of nine. We sent

a violet her first month clean: deeply braided
basket of moss. Desiccated sponge.

The Toothmakers' Daughter, Marking Time

One year since I wrung myself out
like a towel, I dream that a friend is

losing her face to leprosy while I nurse
a lukewarm beer. Hot where before

I was hungry, I wish beyond
my own happiness for the chance

to refuse this: my friend's cheek
a wasteland, and a green bottle,

glinting or clouded in low light.
How it rises to my lips, how I miss

and chip a doorway out of my own smile.

The Toothmakers' Daughter, Teething

Only one wisdom tooth, lower left,
number 17. So slow growing I thought
it would never show. The dentist shook

his head: evolved, not witless. At 33,
known pain I'd forgotten, and they couldn't
help this time if I let them. Half erupted,

half impacted, left so long to grow that removal
involves risk: partial paralysis, broken jaw,
mouth sewn shut with wire.

Decampment

Above the barn, the vane's still a thoroughbred.
Mid-gallop, not canter, and rusted, not russet.
The wind blows North and West and North and then

solely West. Downstairs, my rabbit dug her way out
of the stall years ago, and upstairs, what they call
retirement looks more like a fold. Our father can

no longer breathe. His lungs slip covers in need
of ironing after a life of inhalation: various herbs
set aflame, and fine silt from the grinding wheels.

Their last mouth-less bridges, disembodied, lay
quiet in their clasping boxes, most unfinished.

Divergence

Our parents loved excess and everyone knew:
all the toothless old ladies in town, aware of the weight

of our clinking trash. Today, I live in a one-room apartment
the size of a book. And where is my sister? Hungary,

Singapore, some city where English acts as second tongue.
Her smile remains unblemished as resume paper. Last month,

the hygienist, tow-headed as we were as children, pored
over my x-rays and, aghast, asked, *what happened?*

Sobriety

Three of us abstinent now, one of us dead and all of us
silent. The toilet's ringed with rust, and our skin,
in well water, still smells of old eggs left to sun.

It does not matter where or how far we go. We will
never be free of the family yard. Even when Mother
sells the house to join her new husband (whose dentures

our father mocked while the air left the room of his
body, while death, approaching him, took too long
for all involved parties). Months give way to the flight

of migratory geese. Father, one half of a double plot
that will never now be twinned, no longer calls our names
above the rowdy discord of their bolting, light-tight throats.

The Toothmakers' Daughter, Returning

From beneath the red barn, an endless, dusty stream
of moths spills, stupefied, returning always to the dark,
uninhabited under-source.

The peach trees outside are in fruitless, profuse bloom.
I give. I'd give my eye teeth tonight for family, a long,
tight row of flickering luminaries.

Katherine Fallon attended Salem and Bryn Mawr Colleges, and received her MFA from Sarah Lawrence. Her work has appeared or is forthcoming in *Colorado Review, Meridian, Oxidant Engine, Birds Piled Loosely,* and *Cleaver Magazine,* among others. She is a Lecturer in the Department of Writing & Linguistics at Georgia Southern University, where she bewilderingly teaches a coeducational student body. Katherine resides with her favorite human and a variety of animals, furry and otherwise. She writes to honor memory and to collect the small, daily awarenesses often lost to grocery lists.

CPSIA information can be obtained
at www.ICGtesting.com
Printed in the USA
BVHW070008101118
532734BV00002B/72/P

9 781635 347630